Bus Stop P

by

Gillian Rathbone

Whitehill Publishing

Published by:
Whitehill Publishing
Just Services
Beaumont Enterprise Centre
Boston Road
Beaumont Leys
Leicester LE4 1HB
Tel: 0116 2293102
Email: justandwhitehill@yahoo.com

ISBN 0-9525838-6-0

Gillian Rathbone has long been a wordsmith. Having graduated from the University of Bangor in 1969, she was employed by Oxford University Press. Here she spent five years as a lexicographer and editorial assistant on the Shorter Oxford Dictionary and five more years as an assistant editor in the Educational Reference Book Department. Later, working freelance with two fellow lexicographers, she compiled the Macmillan Learner's Dictionary. She has had local and natural history articles published in Oxford Times Limited Edition magazine and has won several short story competitions.

Gillian began writing poetry four years ago and describes her work as unpretentious. Through her poems, she points to people's foibles without malice or judgement. Her characters come alive in such a way that you find them inhabiting your mind and catch yourself pondering further upon their eccentricities.

For a while, Gillian Rathbone lived in Philadelphia, which she found beautiful but she longed for England. She now lives in the historic city of Oxford, has a love of foreign films, enjoys singing, London, Buxton and the Peak District, Radio 3 and 4, and 19th century literature and music, especially classical symphonic and baroque.

Whitehill Publishing is delighted to present Gillian Rathbone and her "Bus Stop" collection.

Editorial Team
Whitehill Publishing

Contents

At the bus stop

Royal Progress

Beneath a hood
impervious to water
kingbaby flexes
dimpled fists
on this his
unofficial tour
while the
entourage of one
throws her
weight against
the driving rain
unpanoplied

Acceptance

the red-haired Spanish lady
told me at the bus stop
of her seventeen-year-old cat
she'd taken yesterday to the vet's;
smiling she wiped her tears to say
'We left him where he slept'.

Captive audience

a man with features
jumbled up mid-face
came into the shelter,
put up a foot
to fasten a shoe,
then turned to us two –
me and the lady with
the yellow chill bag –
Forty years ago they
abolished the cane
now there's more violence
than ever before –
on which note he left
and the 39 came

All that's chivalric

The air's quite gentle today
lapping her cheeks
as she waits
in the winter
of her resistance

until surprised by desire
as he passes
face gridironed at one side
in angry red patches
yet focused and tall
bearing his scars
unaware of the blaze he's created

in a girl at once reconciled
to all that's chivalric
in the coming of spring

Shop-window hippo

I could envisage
him swimming
unfazed through
an African lake,
a kind of
pipe-smoking type
with port-in-storm jaw
so reassuring
after sampling
the heady pleasure
of a Lothario figure –
often thin-faced.
What a difference
a chin makes.

The fat woman

The fat woman
sways down the street
when her mobile
claims her attention
yet though she
immediately
halts
her flesh
travels on
unrelenting.

Highlight

a can clanks along
the silent street,
glinting in the sun;
on its coming to a stop
I will it to roll on.

Chain of being

eating on the hoof
feeding his face
with greasy fingers
and I grieved
for myself being
distanced from
the angels

All the time in the world

He had all the time
in the world
the man smoking a pipe
on a bench in the station
in a yellow September
till becoming aware
of a chill in the air
when he'd leave
for lawns sloping
down to rock gardens
a drink before dinner
et cetera et cetera
and later on Sunday
he'd shake hands with the vicar
(at Harrow together)
and very soon after
stroll down to the station
there to sit patient
just waiting.

The milkman and the old codger

My dear man -
(incidentally, splendid van!) -
Please don't make a fuss;

this mistiness of morning,
together with
a certain aberrance of retina …
and I mistook you for
          the London omnibus.

The bus depot

It's the sort of place
where boys might kick a ball around –
the only open ground
in a nineteenth-century brown
        house-scape –
where nothing seems to quicken
beneath a massive woollen sky
and the only option is A to B,
a back-and-forth infinity.

Only birds

A blackbird crossed my path
sprang up to a branch
oblivious of anyone
then was gone –
I thought of the squire's only daughter
the lark-catcher who loved her
the birds escaping
to circle her head singing
as if they concurred –
when after all
they were only birds.

A patch of black

In Brasenose Lane
the smell of sausage
emanates from
kitchen gratings
swirls around
a patch of black
less of substance
than the odour
burning up
the air and him.

Country bus stop

The smoking, pine-sweet
            odour of creosote
and in a flash she's six again
by the treated timbers of
            the hen-house -
her shirtless father crossing
            sunless concrete
bird-carcass swinging from a fist,
while her mother at the kitchen door
sensibilities on edge
affects an air of cool disdain,
her only dared rebellion.

Black Dog
in the Bus Shelter

Cowering
in a dusty corner –
your eyes
are my father's
after she died;
shocking to me,
rooted in
a cruel childhood.

Waiting for the last bus
outside the harp shop

Palely
the light
fingers the harp
in the window
and draws me
unwilling
to the
company of others
diminishing into
spectral recesses
where
cold marble
is guarded
by bearers
of flowers
and the
innocent dead
glissando
for hours and hours

Waiting with another generation

Spindly stalks support
clumps of fluffy-looking flowers –
a plant that in times past
Britons used for face-painting
so as to frighten;
their women not to be outdone
painted themselves all over for fun.

We insert pigment beneath
         the epidermis –
     painful, but said to be worth it.

White Cow

Her shape the earliest learned,
though often these days
                    from the page,
a white cow swings her head
knee-deep in a silence
                    that's filled
with the first and best
                    of the world.

On the bus

The first duty of a poet

"to be clinically minded was …
the first duty of a poet".
C. Isherwood 1937

The Breughel clown,
place behind a plough,
with doughy face
gives out small grunts
until his stop
then stands
knees bent
as if
to negotiate a slope and
grips the pole
uncertainty urgent
in his soul.

The woman in front

Encased in
something synthetic
she wears her hair
like a cut-down busby
so black and matt
you'd swear it was bearskin

and I think of
a hussar
in braided jacket
dolman of scarlet
hung like a cape
from one shoulder
scouring the plain
in every direction

and when she turns
I find her eyebrows
denuded either
with pitiless pincers
or drawn up remorseless
into the surprise
of that hair.

The last bus

On the brewing-up bus
he peered bifocally down
at the tabloid before him –
Lifting the Lid on Sin City –
their doing away
with National Service
had turned out more than a pity.

Sense of direction

in shirt Aztec-checked,
he rounds the hole in the road,
then swaying to a halt
confronts a traffic cone –
unaware, perhaps, it's not
withholding information
as to where he is.

Red carnations

She wasn't over-keen on
             most carnations,
equating them with business suits,
weddings of the boring sort.
Flesh-coloured, white, she'd shudder
             at such colours,
even pinks showed
a kind of paucity of spirit.
Yet a red carnation she could
             happily relate to,
suggesting as it did some
             endeavour to become
all that she applauded in a flower.

This predilection her admirers
were quick to cotton onto –
in their proper season red carnations
             filled her house;
so much so, she could have
             spent her time in
eating them by the dozen.

What a way to go
(with thanks to Graham Greene)

As when the teacher
forced to inform a pupil
his father'd been killed
by a pig in Italy
falling on his head
from a verandah,
so the girl cyclist
when a chubby vehicle
marking yellow lines
did a sudden U-turn -
the near collision with her
and her laughter
bordering on hysteria.

Stiff upper lip

Weighted down with
           bulging suitcase
Dripping in rain-soaked clothes
I ask the driver for the station

And wonder why I collude
           with a smile
When he informs me with a
           sort of joy
That's way past his destination.

Humps

What came across was
his excess of energy
his bright-eyed alertness
as we paid our fares –
and the way he took off
hurtling a passenger
right down the bus …
and those wretched road humps
how people grumbled –

all far from the usual
morning inertia
of going-to-workers.

The old values

As with my grandpa
rising for the Queen's speech
getting there when it's nearly complete

so with the old gentleman -
my stopping place fast coming up -
finally offering his seat on the bus.

Set in daylight

I dwell on how I like to be scared.
Things graphic don't do it –
apparitions and violence –
there's the adrenaline rush
but I need something other –
so the review of a thriller
about reincarnation
'it's the scariest ever
despite set in daylight'
is guaranteed to appeal.

Yet … funny how someone
can appear to embody another;
take this cold-eyed lady
settling beside me
she's the absolute spit
of that bullying teacher
so much so that I study
Christmas lights over Broad Street
and decide they'll look pretty
in the evening when lit.

Street graffiti

newly tarmacked,
the road seems
strangely bare;
you're talking
yellow lines,
he said,
as he took my fare.

Needs must

We bus people peered with interest
as the bag lady in rusty coat and hood
swooped to a bin and
raised a carton to her lips
took a swig
swirled it around
and downed it –
all to our oh no kind of sound.
She's not squeamish is she?
someone said;
which pretty well sums up
what we thought about it,
we people on the bus.

Tattooed woman

She just makes it
and flops down
face lined with sweat
giving me glances
to collude in her
skin of teeth feat
and I shrink into
a half smile
from this woman
smelling of pee
arms tattoed a
dirty purple and blue
as if she and her
markings could
somehow stain me
and at the next stop
I'm left to
deal with the
shame that erases
any relief I might feel

Overheard on the bus

38

Don't sit next to me!

She was on the bus today
the woman with the loud posh voice.
Don't you think the
city centre's a disgrace –
workmen everywhere
practically a no-go area.
And look at that –
as we neared the business school –
no aesthetic values
anywhere;
take that woman at the Tate
the one whose dirty knickers
won the Turner prize –
at which point
I'm almost sure
An old man upped and died.

Who was he to say?

With compassion-laden
conversation
the shopping-trollied
pious couple
board the local bus.
'I'm very much afraid to say
Margaret's wasted her entire life' –
and that is all
for important matters
occupy his wife.
Nonetheless I am indignant –
Who was he to say? -
Take a look at your own, you prick,
before you write hers away.

The dog-lover

'Dogs is a delicacy
out there' she said
waving a crutch
toward Europe
'they'll eat dogs
soon as look at you' -
and here gave a shudder –
on which someone
comfy in four-ply
piped up 'and snails'!
a remark met with
the flick of a ticket stub
into the gutter

Loss of face

'Four legs, four letters,
beginning with E' –
she put forward eagle
then in confusion
urged him – tell me

(yes hurry, I thought,
my stop's coming up –
without knowing
I can't leave the bus)

but he wouldn't say –
was it the case
he'd got the wrong spelling
in the first place?

Every man I meet

In shape a Margaret Rutherford
except atop the comic looks
a gorgeous wedding sort of hat
pink and gauze and delicate
which she was bent on propping up
the better to survey the bus
and announce to all and sundry
Every man I meet – he wants me!

When silence is golden

Our bus driver tells us
'Won't be a minute'
getting out at the depot
while we wait in silence
till the sharp-nosed old woman
declares it's disgusting!
with an emphatic stab of her cane.

Eyeing the skewer
keeping her hat on
I decide an answer
would be nothing gained.

Oh no

Oh no!

I looked behind;
a woman, eyes half-smiling,
                scandal-bright.

It's this –
she shook the pages of the
                Oxford Mail –
near where I live
a body found last night
I wondered what was going on.

She read further;
I asked – A murder?

Oh no –
flicking over, face composed –
Just a hit-and-run.

A view from the bus

Jack the Lad

Putting up two fingers
to the public
offering anyone
a shag
that's Jack the lad,
swigging, gigging,
radio on full blast –
how I want him to
make music of his own.

Christmas in Oxford

A brawl had broken out
at traffic lights
and standing on the bus
waiting to get off
we watched a tourist
skirt the scrum
stop on the crossing
and take a photograph.

Perspective

Beneath blue-white
fast-moving skies
the tunnel looms
where day after day
commuters are consumed
and then let go –
where light encounters darkness
at dawn and sunset.

It's as if some thing passes

Along lanes curving
in a valley formed by college walls
there's a sense of presence
where a deed unspeakable occurred
behind studded double doors –
it's as if some thing passes,
driven hooves
that jostle up a spectral dust.

At an open window

A man smokes at an open window
shirt-sleeved, bald,
while near a dark-wood dresser,
with a murky carafe of water,
his wife in sateen slip
sits reading sprawled.

The day awaits
though there's no rush to use it
and when the chamber-maid comes in
to fix the bed
he'd tell her
we'll be out soonish.

Turning point

Like a bead running loose
from a broken chain,
the child in ankle-length black
strays across the white street
and takes the hand
of a black-coated stranger
and follows to where
the mother quickens
from some brink to pure joy;

while the stranger
will ponder on that bright place
until at last she asks why
and arrives face to face
with her self,
accepting as prize
with its attendant emptiness
the turning aside.

A summer night

Framed in a hotel window
she idles sideways at a piano
dark-haired, in cherry-red
that's orange-tinted in the room's
harsh light;
and I wonder at what
a few notes can do
in the stillness
of a summer night.

Top of the bus

Cultivated fields
of purple broccoli
turn out to be
banks of bicycles
shining under
an Indian summer sun.

Running into summer

As the bus draws to
a halt
three young girls
arms free
short-sleeved
faces bright
tumble out
to where
shadowless pleasures
appear to
await

across the
broad white pavement
running into summer
as fast as their heels
can carry them.

Flashback

golden bowl
of oranges
catching the sun –
globes flashing amber –
she pauses
before proceeding

Indoor Games

It was like the picture on a
             jigsaw-puzzle lid;
a timber cottage –
tended lawns
inside a lead-blue wall
niched for languid statues –
all beneath a geniality of sky.

Thinking jigsaws took her back
to snakes and ladders,
and a mother sulky-shouldered –
so that, even when she won,
victory was hollow.

Yet, after all, in terms of
the philosophy of India
(the game's origins are there),
the extinction of desire and passion,
letting go the solid 'I',
lie off the board.

Whereas with that cottage and its ilk -
despite sometimes the anxiety of sky -
on completion of assembly
came the illusion of control
and an evenness of mind
for a time.

Country Living

With narrowed vision
through
shimmering lawns
and
spangled spray
in the sunlight
of privilege
she plans her day.

Red Legs

as a species
he's not threatened;
as a partridge
he's fair game.

Bus journeys

Nostalgia

A fickle breeze
fingerprints a
silver stretch
of river
causes
moored boats
to fan out
and lightly lands
on the broad branches
of a stately fir
testing coyly
for buoyancy

A chameleon reflects

Just imagine, if you can,
being able to change
the colour of your skin,
infiltrate any situation
unobserved;
my ability to go from
yellow through to inky blue
quite suits my temperament –
inanimate in general.
Call me inconstant, even fickle
                    if you will –
I'll not be fazed;
to take offence needs energy
and, like this poem, I'm
                    not going
any place.

Limbo

the bus was
above sea-level
the road sloping to
drenched fields
and as the driver
plunged into
the blurry landscape
she supposed he was
entirely focused
that things looked
differently
from where he was

Open-topped bus

That whitestone lighthouse
where an ageing fair-ground actress
at the close of the racket
when the lights were shut down
gave herself up to hope
and the sea's dull roaring.

Rolling along

Over soft
brown country
where a
stream's in spate
and a horse paws
impatient at the wait
beneath trees

En route for Ludlow

A Shropshire village;
Coal fires and
Toasting forks of brass.

Thick white silence stuns.
No footprints track the blue lane
Alongside the frozen stream;
Snow fields are lost in an opaque sky.

Her childhood brought
The Snow Queen;
Trusting in silvery embraces
And sleigh bells
Singing false promises.

At the day's end

Where
slender-limbed
marsh grasses
rise up in
flooded flat lands
is home for
a V of geese
flying in from a
yellow-streaked
vesper sky.

Excursion

The spoiling weather
the line of deckchairs
drawn back beneath trees
it's what they'd all expected
and when one pronounces
This is what I paid good money for
after a brief consensus of opinion
inertia is resumed once more.

Read on a journey home

after a day's fishing
in a synchronized dance
bent bills level with
the Equator
lines of flamingos unite;
they may be treading
a grave and stately measure
to their own music
even as I write.

Sarcophagus

fragments of
gold-threaded
damask silk –
how it would
shimmer
when she moved

Outing to the Pavilion Gardens, Buxton

Giving the lie to
paddling feet
they glide and take
the centre of the lake
indifferent to
undercover scufflings
of moorhens in
reedy margins;
as white as clouds
they're above all that.

Day trip to Brighton

He brylcreemed, waits to be fed,
while his spouse in her 'good' coat
inspects her back of hand, its
                wedding ring –
until a waitress nears
to hover on a hip –
when she, the lady wife
darting from the girl's condition
to the grubby unringed finger
allows a grim smile of satisfaction.

Confidences

actually a snapshot, sepia,
torn a bit across and
found in the bottom of a box
of loose photographs
to be sorted out;
soldier-straight
he stands behind
compliant wife
she'll learn it's wise to smile
when being sorted out.